I0450110

The Overcomer

From Past to Present

by

Sunshine

authorHOUSE®

AuthorHouse™
1663 Liberty Drive
Bloomington, IN 47403
www.authorhouse.com
Phone: 833-262-8899

Published by AuthorHouse 09/25/2020

ISBN: 978-1-4259-8346-8 (sc)

Print information available on the last page.

This book is printed on acid-free paper.

Thank you Lord, for every time you've saved me and kept me from hurt and harm. I now praise you for being the compassionate God you are. One who guides my life today in every way?

Evangelist Mary Quick

-In memory of Ruby Inzar who believed in her granddaughter that no matter what I've done throughout my life God loves me for just who I am. I thank God for all of her many prayers.

This is dedicated to all the women of present and past abuse. Just when you think all hope is lost and feel like you cannot come out of the situation just look at me. I over came through it all. I can do all things through God that strengthens me.

Acknowledgements

First, I would like to thank God the father my lord and savior Jesus Christ. There was always a time I was tired from writing but the Holy Spirit kept saying to me this is for someone who is going through abuse right now and needs a way out letting them know that they are not alone.

My loving husband Bernard who stands beside me because he knows if God gives it to me I will follow through and do it. My children Aja, Shatrece, and David who said mommy we are behind you all the way and my two grandchildren Jakai and Jazzy. Nana loves you both very much.

Living Epistle Bible College: Dean Bishop Dr. Tyrone Hunter for teaching me that a minister does more than preach. If God gives it that settles it, ministry is about winning souls. Minister Gunn from Living Epistle Bible College who always listens to me as I tell my story and encouraged me to go ahead and write my autobiography.

"Beautiful Women"

Arise Beautiful women arise dry those weary and dreary eyes.
There will be no more tears; there will be no more pain.
All your spots have been washed clean away.
Look no more to your left or your right.
Look straight ahead into Gods beam of glowing lights.
So, let go and start to grow because now you don't have
To look back anymore.

Evangelist Mary Quick

As far back as I can remember growing up was fun we only had each other to play with. Ruby, Robert and Roe, Rose, and I created our own games for fun. Me and my sister Ruby we would pretend that we had this long hair and live in the luxurious homes. As we got older I had found new friends outside of my siblings. Their names were Cindy and Lisa. Cindy was the baby girl in her family and stayed on the fourth floor; my mom would let me and Ruby go down to play with her from time to time. Now Lisa was bossy. She always wanted me play with her all the time and every chance she got she would pull me away from Cindy. My father didn't live with us. My mom and dad separate a while back. 7th floor Mission Hill Projects was what my mom and step dad called home. Weekends were great we took trips to the beach or taking family outing, visiting with my step dad coworker from the post office. Even though we grew up in the projects our lives were mold not to become the project Life as a young child was good; we didn't want or need for anything. My mom always tried to make sure that our needs were met. I remember my mother getting a call one day from my aunt in North Carolina saying that my father had died. I was around 13 years old. I will never forget that day. We were told that he had been sick had car accident. The car crashed into a bridge. He had passed out and ran straight into it. That was a very painful experience for me. He was on his way to see us before we left to spend the summer with my great grandmother.

That was the worst summer I ever had; there were so much funeral preparations to be made. I remember going to view the body, my father, William Grice, looked so peaceful in his final resting place. Now thinking about it I hope he gave his life to God for salvation so that I will see him again. It was nice visiting with family members, each time I see my aunts on my fathers side they would always get very spoiled. I don't get to see them as often as I should. I felt much love from them. After the burial we went back and fellowshipped with everyone, the next day it was over, William Grice dead in the year of 1974. Returning back to the life I knew without my daddy at the age of 13. I was very sad because I didn't' get much time to spend with him.

Colossians 3:5, 8-10

Therefore put to death your members which are on earth: fornication, uncleanness, passion, evil desire, and covetousness, which are adultery." Verse 8 says "but know you yourselves are to put off all these: angel, wrath, malice, blasphemy, filthy language out of your mouth." Verse 9 says "do not lie to one another, since you have put off the old man with his deeds." A verse 10 says "and have on the

It is said that each family has a generation curse. Well I guess maybe its true or you just mimic what you saw as a child growing up because I can remember my mother and father always fighting. There was a lot of yelling and hitting, once my father hit my mom to the point where she passed out. He then had asked me to get some water and I did, when she awoke he left. I think that was the last I really saw of him. There are some things that stay with you and you never forget them as much as you may want too.

I still loved my father and really miss him very much; maybe my life would have taken a different turn if I had a loving father in my life. I needed that kind of a relationship to show me how a happy family should be. When my father left there were other men in my mother's life but not a real father figure. The facade of the Cosby show was what I dreamed of; not what I lived. My mother met my stepfather, Money, about four of dealing with the Wong men in and out of her life. He was the closest thing to a dad that I could remember since the passing of my biological father. The other men just came when it was convenient for their needs. We moved out a nice area and into the projects. I always had a good heart and my friends always new 1 was true to them. I finally got interested in boys it took a while because I was afraid, I know that sounds crazy. I thought all that wanted was sex from me.

When my sister, Ruby, and I started going out more she would be the most popular with the boys. There was one boy, Percy; he was the meanest person that I ever came in contact with. He would always call me ugly names: "black as tar" or "blacky" and so on. After a while you get tired of being called out of your name. I wanted so bad to say something to Percy but I was too scared to speak up for myself. One day I just got feed up my surroundings. I let Percy define me. He told me who I was. I was now believing that I was these things: ugly, didn't have a backbone, couldn't fight. I felt like the ugly duckling, no friends. I was tired. I was going to end it all. I had a bottle of pills. I was going to do it; the unthinkable. No one would miss me. Not even my own mama. What do I have to live for? I took at least twenty pills from a bottle and thought to myself this is it. I'm going to do it. I'll just end it all and won't have to hear anymore Perry's in my life. A child handles being bullied in different ways. I was thinking that I was going to take the easy way out. A lot of them retaliate, or kill themselves because it hurts so bad and they feel like they can't go on taking the pain. I hid the pills in my dresser. That night I got a glass of water and retrieved the pills from the dresser drawer. I took one pill and could not take another one. I don't know why until this day. A thought came in my mind that he's going to continue call me these names whether I was dead of alive. I overcame Perry. I figured it wasn't my time to go or just not like that, God had something for me to accomplish and I am still doing them.

Psalm 37:1-4 do not fret because evil doers, nor envious of the workers of iniquity: for they shall soon be cut down like grass, and wither as the green herb: trust in the Lord, and do good dwell in the land and feed on his faithfulness: delight yourself also in the Lord and he shall give you the desires of your heart.

I grew up into a well groomed lady but still I was always shy and kept to myself. When I met Thomas we talked on the phone a lot because my mom really didn't want me to start dating yet. If a young man would come over we'll sit in the living room and watch TV and talk until she said he had to leave. I had many male friends that my mother new was just that and nothing more and she was okay with that. One day she allowed Thomas to visit and she went outside to sit and social drink.

We were alone one thing led to another and things happened. I can't remember were my brother and sisters were at some how we ended up in my mother's room. That was the first I had ever been with a man, I was 17 years old. That one time got me pregnant. Now once I found out that I was pregnant the part that scared me was how to tell my mother. I knew my mother would be upset with me because my art career was taking off and I was going to try out modeling. I didn't tell I packed my bags one morning like I was going to school and ran away from home. In doing so my life went downhill after, it became a nightmare.

I showed up at Thomas' door and told him I was pregnant and ran away from home because I was scared to tell my mother. I wasn't sure what was going through his mind but there's when all my self-esteem went down hill. I am telling you this because a man can take a bad situation and use it to his advantage. He had turned me into his personal slave and isolated me from my family and friends. A man can turn you out and have you frostbiting your body knowing that you are scared and will do anything to keep from going home. I moved in with Thomas and had rules to follow just like a child.

My schedule was to go to school come home and go right into the bedroom and stay there until he got home. When I started showing; I stopped going to school until after I had my daughter, Andrea. While Thomas was at work all I could do was look out the window or watch TV. I could only leave the room to use the bathroom. I was mostly home by myself while his mom and step dad worked. His younger sister was in school and the other one was pregnant too. Thomas told me that she was on drugs.

I was told to stay away from her and not to talk to her. Well at first I wouldn't say much but after a while I started conversation with her because I had missed communicating with other people. It's human nature to talk to others. His sister's name was Tasha. Sometimes she would say things to me like "I know how my brother is and I know he said not to talk to me; but its okay if you do". Tasha would say so many negative things about her brother and the rest of the family. When her baby's father would come over I would over hear them arguing; it was always about money issues. I figured he knew her situation and her stormy relationship with her mother and would use it to his advantage.

She never told me but I knew he was using her for prostitution. I use to hear her crying but I didn't know what to do. I was in a relationship where I was being mentally abused also. I knew if I couldn't help myself ....how I could help someone else. Some days when Thomas came home I was allowed to leave the bedroom and go to the kitchen and cook for us. At night when I had to use the bathroom I would get out of the bed while Thomas was sleeping and pee in a cup that I placed under the bed. One day I got tired of feeling like I'm in freed prisoner. One early I tell you I got myself together and I packed a few things when Thomas went to work. I ran away to run away back where I started from.

Thomas would come and get me to bring me right back. Instead of telling him no; I went back with him each and every time. There were so many of these episodes that I lost count. That was the type of strong hold he had on me. It was like I was under a spell and couldn't break free from it. I returned to my prison room once again. Now through our time together I never addressed him by his first name. I don't know why but I always called him "King" that was his last name. Life went on the same and on weekends we went to the park and sat around like all the men and their wives or girlfriends were doing.

Thomas would talk with the other men and women I would just sit there and look lost. I never really said much anyways. When we were in the car I was never allowed to look out the window because he would say I was looking for another man. I just looked straight ahead or held my head down.

Colossians 1:27-28 "to them God willed to make known what are the riches of the glory of this mystery among the gentiles: which is Christ in you, the hope of glory. The next verse says "him we preach, warning every man and teaching every man in all wisdom, that we may present every man perfect in Christ Jesus.

In April of 1979 our daughter, Rea, was born. She was a very small baby due to being born premature. Once, I brought her home life for us didn't change. Believe it or not it got worse. Now I had a baby that was just as confined as I was. One evening Thomas brought home some purple and black pills. I can remember taking one and feeling spaced out, nervous, and all shaky. I didn't know if I was coming or going. I was so glad when I start coming down off the drug where I could function again. I thank God the baby never woke up during that time. Well let's put it like this she was sleep when I alert of my surroundings. .

One summer day I can remember it being very hot. I awoke out of a deep sleep and found my baby girl in the window crying. She had crawled out to the edge of the window. I was so scared when I saw her out there. I snatched her back into the house and by the grace of God my child didn't fall out of the sixth floor window that had no screen and was wide open. I know that it had to be angels there holding her. I thank God for saving my child. I believe that she was crying for a long time because her eyes were very red. I never again allowed myself to sleep so heavy anymore.

After living with his family for a while we finally moved out, I had gotten a job and my mother was keeping Rea. Thomas and I were having so many problems. I was being mentally abused until one day it became physical. I lost my job and didn't know how to tell Thomas. Each day I acted like I was going to work until payday came and Thomas wanted to know where my money was and I told him that I had lost it. He made me empty out my whole pocket book to search for that money all night long.

When he said that I could finally go to bed I was so relieved and scared at the same time. I just knew that wanted to hit me; but he didn't. It's amazing how I looked for monies that I knew never existed. Thomas sound asleep. I remembered packing me and my babies' clothes at three o'clock in the morning. I put my coat on and started walking to my mother's house. She lived very far; but I was scared and I knew I couldn't stay there any longer. We walked so long and she was so heavy I didn't know if we were going to make it. A police officer came by and asked why I was out so late at night with a baby and where I was going. He called my mother and took me and my child to her house and there I stayed.

Deuteronomy 31:6 "be strong and of good courage, do not fear nor be afraid of them, for the Lord your God, he is the one who goes with you and he will not leave you nor forsake you.

Thomas came and tried to get me to come back. This time I was determined that I was not going. He became so angry that he threw a brick into my mother's window and ran away. I started focusing on getting my life back together. I had found a good job working at a retail store and was doing very well. I met Mike and we became good friends. Mike introduced me to his brother, Lyle. We dated for a while; he was living with his mother, father, sister and three brothers. We became very close that I started having overnight visits with him and Rea now eight was staying with my mom. Now would you believe that it happened again? I became pregnant. I thought to myself here we go again.

When I told my mother that I was pregnant you've should have known that she wasn't happy about it. My mother was so angry she threatened to knock the baby right out of my stomach. Due to an argument we had within a week I found a place in Roslindale. The apartment was nice, it was a two bedroom. Eventually, my mom and I were back on speaking terms. I had furnished it all on my own. Soon after Lyle moved in with me; that's really when the problems started. I say to you ladies "Don't let a man move in with you or you move in with him unless you are married". Lyle already had two children but they stayed with their mother. I found out that he was still creeping to see her. Yet, I still stayed with him anyway. I worked until ray ninth month of pregnancy. Lyle was living with me but buying pot and paying bills with his disability check at his mom house.

I stayed home thinking I was going to have the baby but she was three weeks over due. When Tracey was born her father was at the amusement park with his family. Throughout our relationship I knew he was cheating on me but I really didn't care. 1 was letting Lyle's ex-girlfriend do my hair and not knowing that she was shooting up. At that time I was snorting cocaine and smoking marijuana. Lyle smoked all the time everyday. I had gone back to work and Lyle was keeping the kids and when I got home he went to hang out with the boys. One day I decided to go out with a girl friend from work while my mom babysat the kids for me.

We went to a bar and had a great time. I met a man that sold cocaine and gave it to me all night long. You should know that nothing is free in this world. I didn't go home that night. I ended up going home with this guy from the bar. We went to one of his female friend's apartment. The next morning I went home and Lyle was there with his sister and her husband packing clothes. He had picked up Tracey from mammas and left Rea. He told me that he was taken his daughter with him. I didn't let take anything including my child from the apartment. Guess what ladies men can leave and stay out all night long; but when you do it is a whole different story. Lyle came back that night like nothing ever happened. Pete, the guy from the bar called and Lyle answered the phone. He was upset and he started choking me and I just knew that he was going to kill me. The baby started to cry and he released the tight grip that he had around my neck. He went in the bedroom and packed his stuff and left. All the time we were together and he was cheating on me but when the tables turned around it was a conflict

Psalm 31:9-16

A month went by and Lyle would send money for the baby. I had found that out that Lyle was seeing my neighbor who was supposed to be my friend. It was late one evening and Tracey wasn't even a year old, I sent my oldest daughter to get a cigarette from Leona. She saw Lyle sitting at my friend's apartment. That's how I found out that they had been seeing each other. I guessed that they had been seeing each other while I was at work. How much of a dog can you be to go right next door and cheat?

Well Lyle and I stop talking and the only thing we had to talk about was the baby. He loved his daughter very much. The next door neighbor and I never spoke again. I continued to see my friend from the bar every weekend. He still continued to give me my special package. He was selling at the bar and it got to the point where everyone knew who I was. I was now buying cocaine and always wanted that taste. Sometimes I would put it my cigarettes or just snort it before work. All I know is I could get it easy.

Now even though I had my drug friend I still continued to talk to other guys. I can recall a man named James that liked me. We use to flirt a lot and would see each other after work and yes soon I was sleeping with him off and on. One day we just stopped seeing each other because I felt like he wasn't what I wanted. I met another guy he was a fireman and also worked at a retail store part time. Well this man was really nice, he treated me really good and we dated until he wanted to control me. I remember one day at the bar my supplier friend asked me "Have I ever been with a woman"? At first I didn't know what to think or say.

I told him no of course but he said he wanted me to try it. I told him sure we can one day and he picked the woman. She was my buddy whose apartment we had always went to have sex. I knew they use to mess around with each other but I just blocked it out. She really didn't care we were all friends because he was her supplier too. Needless to say we never had the threesome. After a while the fling was over and I didn't see him anymore. At times me and Tracey's father was back and forth with each other but he never moved back in with me.

Galatians 5:1 "stand fast therefore in the liberty by which Christ has made us free and do not be entangled again with a yoke of bondage.

I met an MBTA driver on the trolley one day while going to my mama's to wash my clothes. He asked for my number and yes; I gave it to him. I didn't really think he would call. I guess you can say each relationship I had been in was for comfort or just sex. When he finally did call we went out and he only wanted one thing and you know once they get that then you really don't hear from them any more. After a while I stopped dating and decided to just focus on raising my children. After about two or three months later Lyle and I started dating again. I had moved back with my mother. She had moved out of the Mission Hill projects and moved to Brighton, MA due to renovation of the apartment she was in.

I would go over Lyle's mother or sister's apartment and stay the night at times. After awhile the relationship was over again. I got a job working at the coast guard as a security officer. We were called the security police. I really liked that job because we were in charge of the base. I wasn't dealing with anyone on base except for the manager who was in charge of the security officers. His name was Riley and he was a stern man. He was very good to me. Our first date was at a bar on Huntington Ave. We had drinks and later we went back to my sister's place. You know what happened there.

He was just ending a relationship with a former worker who had kept coming to see him for a while but it finally stopped. I found out that Riley was staying with his sister who really didn't like me at all. She never spoke to me and worked only on the weekends. Riley was a military man. He really lived by those standards. We dated for a very long time. He had met my family and they loved him very much. We went on vacations and he cooked for me. Suddenly our job ended and we were all looking for new ones. Our relationship wasn't going so good around that time. I can truly say that Riley treated me with respect he treated me somewhat like a queen. Yet and still he had things to deal with in his own personal life.

I got a job as security for cable vision, it was a night job. I didn't get off until the next morning. It was an okay job. I had to check the doors through the building to make sure everything was okay and monitor the grounds from the computer. I was the only one working at night. You would think my mind could really do a lot of thinking but noooo, I met this man I can't really remember how it came about, we hung out did our thing. It got to the point when he was coming to the job to hang out with me. We were doing other things there as well like getting high and having sex.

Now each morning as the technicians were coming in there was this guy who kept watching me. He seemed nice and soon after he gave me his phone number. I was still seeing Travis. James and I started going out a lot. It seems that every man I met were into drugs and doing cocaine. I started really liking James and finally he took me to his place on Beacon St. where he shared his apartment with a roommate named J.D. We all hit it off great then I found out that he was a drug dealer.

Well you know that doesn't make matters better because it's like going backward. Remember I was dating a drug dealer in the beginning of my story. Well needless to say he was feeding me free drugs all over again. Even though James and I were seeing each other on a regular basis I was still hanging out Travis. Tragedy hit the family. My great grandmother died. We had to go to N.C. for the funeral but I just started a job so I couldn't go. That really hurt me because I loved my grandmother Mary a lot. So I stayed behind and worked while the family was gone. I was lucky that my mother took my two girls with her because she was my only babysitter at night.

While the family was gone for the weekend I hung out with James and J.D. and all we did was just stay in and do drugs all weekend. Now a good time passed and I moved in with both men. I didn't know what I was getting myself into but my life was about to change. One day James asked me would I like to make some money on the side, well of course I said yes and that meant leaving my security job. I became an evening woman where men of business would come by and I would do what they wanted. So James had the men come over to the apartment that he, J.D., and I shared.

You see the area we stayed in was a very upper class neighborhood you couldn't get into the apartment without being buzzed in. James had to prepare me earlier before the first male arrived. After everything was over James would come in and talk with me then I showered. James would always say it was for the both of us then he would want to sleep with me. So you see the enemy kept my mind on other things; never on anything positive like going to church or about how Jesus died for me. I was going deeper and deeper into a life style I never really wanted. Then one day James brought this girl over to our home and took her to our bedroom.

James left with the young lady and returns home alone. Of course he tried to say they were just friends or something to that effect. He came clean and told me that he and the girl is getting married and trying to buy a house. By this time J.D. was now asking if he could offer me a proposition, he would give me a certain amount of drugs to have sex with him. I was hooked to drugs so I took the offer. I felt bad and I really didn't want to do this. Later I ran into Riley and he told me about a job in the Veteran Administration as a secretary. I filled the papers out and got the job. I got a job as a secretary and wasn't at the job a year before I decided to go spend the weekend in New Jersey with a man. I started seeing another man at the Veterans Administration which Riley didn't approve of. This seemed like it would be a new start for me. J.D. was moving out going back to New York and asked if I would take over the payments for rent. He paid it up for about two months.

Well it didn't last that long again with Riley and me. I was flirting with this man and this really bothered Riley. He became very upset with me. James still kept in touch at times and then one day the family had to go to New Jersey for my aunt's funeral which was my grandmother's sister. Now by this time I was pregnant with Riley's son. He was very happy because this would be his first child and finally that sister of his could stop treating me so evil. They were staying together still and I would always wonder if she was his sister or not. Anyway while we were in New Jersey I met this man named Fred. I can't remember how far along I was in my pregnancy but we exchanged numbers and kept in contact.

You see I was still messed up on that drug cocaine. After we returned Riley and I still were having problems. Soon we drifted apart for good but he still wanted to do right by his son. That type of bond kept us together. You see we both had problems with drugs that needed to be worked out. You cannot come together with issues that heavy and think that everything is going to be okay. Now Tracey's father came back into the picture. I was about eight and a half months and we started dating again. While carrying my son it also brought me closer to my mother. I was on leave we did a lot of things together up until my son was born. My son was born on October 4, 1987 and through him I stopped doing drugs. On the day I went into labor it was a hard time I felt like this was payback for everything I had done. After a while Riley left the Veterans Administration but I stayed on. I had a casual relationship with an orderly. .

There were lots of times money got stolen from my sister that was on crack cocaine. I can remember meeting a guy from New York and we took a trip to Cape Cod for the weekend. After that we never saw each other again. I guess I was looking for happiness but looking for it in all the wrong places. I didn't know that God could fulfill that empty void in my life. I remember meeting another guy who worked as a cleaner and there were lots of times we just had sex but never at his home or mine.

One day after work I met a man that made me an offer and sad to say I accepted it. My memory tells me he was a lawyer just looking for some action. That lasted for a while you see I kept slipping back into prostitution. I had all these different spirits in my body because once you lay down with someone and you have engaged in a sexual act all the spirits they have on them have entered into you.

I didn't just stop at being a call girl. There was a time when I left work and ran into an old friend at the bus stop. We talked for a very long time before I really made it home. He made another offer and made it sound really good. Since my self-esteem was already low I took it not knowing what was really at hand for me. He explained that I could really make a lot of money and introduced me to one of the girls that worked for him. She made it seem like I could bring in a lot of money. So I was taken out and he brought me outfits and makeup son I could really fix myself up.

I was picked up from home and dropped off on the action corner. I really realized I had become lower than all the things I had done and I wanted out. It was cold and I looked foolish standing on the corner waiting for a trick to come by. When the night was over I had one person and made only twenty-five dollars. I got out of that arrangement right away. Time passed as well as months I still remained at the Veterans Administration. Then one night something happened that changed my life completely around and it took a lot for me to turn it around in one night.

I slept in the living room one hot night. I woke up and saw my sister Roe in the kitchen with her friend. I got up and asked them what they were doing? Remembering that prior year her friend had offered me drugs. Now at first I said "No, I don't want to get hooked on that stuff". Both of them claimed oh no you won't, taste it. Nevertheless, I did. If anyone ever tells you that crack cannot get you hooked they are just telling you lies. All it takes is one inhale and the rush affects your membrane which gives you this high.

All it took was once. I wanted more and more. I end up spending all of money on my habit. I never would go and purchase my drugs. Roe would always go and do it for me. I really started sinking into crack cocaine world. My weight was going fast and the thing about this was no one ever knew what was going on. My family never questioned anything because they I hid my weight loss my wearing pants on top of pants. Time continued to go by and while I was at work no one knew anything. One day the family went out of town to North Carolina to visit my grandmother. Upon returning Roe had sold all my electronic equipment. I was very upset and threatened to take her to court.

My life went on and I was still on crack. Roe got an apartment and I moved in. My oldest daughter stayed with my mother she had moved back to Mission Hill in a two bedroom. My two smaller children were with Roe and I along with her three children. I went to work and Tracey was in school and my son went to my mothers each morning. Paycheck for me was every two weeks. I gave my mother money for pampers and food. The rest of the money went towards for me and Roe. There were times when we didn't have any money to wash clothes so I washed them with soap. Life went on like this for about four years. I tried save monies by leaving money in my desk at work in case an emergency would arise. You see I had advanced from secretary to administrator. I had an office with an assistant to help me do customer discharges.

My sister and I had used all the money we had on drugs. I caught three buses to my job to get my emergency stash. All I did was show my I.D, went to my office, open the door, and got my emergency stash for my emergency. I took the money back to the apartment and Roe went to purchase the drugs. She came back and we got high. This went on until one day I got tired and really started to think about if something was to happen to me who would take care of my kids. We went to go visit my grandmother for a week and it made me realize; I did not do drugs that entire week; maybe I could beat this. When I returned Roe had gotten me again. My big floor model TV was gone and she sold all our food. I really wanted to leave. My cousin had contacted me because she was having problems and wanted to leave Boston. Hey, this was my opportunity to get out also. We set a date and I gave my mother money to hold. I told her not to spend it because my children and I were moving. My grandmother said it was okay for us to stay. Roe thought I wasn't going anywhere. I kept asking her, "What would she do if I left"?

Roe's daughter, Angel, was sucking an empty bottle as if she was getting her nourishment for food. I hated to leave and leave her kids with her because there was no food coming in anymore. What was I to do? I was getting by to take care of me and mine. On the day we were leaving my mom picked me up. Rea didn't want to leave her grandmother and decided to stay with her. We left on the train and I never went back to those drugs again. Once I departed my life in Boston; I always continue to say that was a very happy day in my life but a very sad one in Roe's life. She became pregnant again and all her kids were taken away. To this day she is still on drugs from twenty-two years plus and this is the year 2006.

Jeremiah 30:17 "for I will restore health to you and heal you of your wounds says the Lord."

Now my job was transferred to the VA in North Carolina. I worked there for a good while my cousin had been taken me back and forth until she couldn't do it anymore. I had got in contact with a girl who I carpool with to work. I finally moved into my own apartment it was furnished from a friend that my grandma knew. I had been going to church on Sundays with grandma and partying on the weekends. Grandma didn't mind watching the kids. She taught my son how to use the potty. She was really a life savor and didn't know it or maybe she did. Then one day I can honestly say I found myself at the front of a church crying, confessing my sins and became a candidate for baptism.

I was baptized Mother's Day and I have been saved ever since. Now that road wasn't easy because while working at the VA I met a nice man who was also saved. We had lunch and became friends then dated. Now everything was fine and I was maintaining my newfound life until one day. We both slipped and really I think that changed our relationship. Paul would visit but never stayed overnight. Rea came too lived in NC with Tracey, Don and I. We were finally a family. I was living a good life until I found out Paul got married and didn't tell me. He wanted to keep our relationship going. That really hurt but it was the only reason he could give me. I moved on and repented before the church. Each time I sinned I asked for forgiveness. I feel like I could have died so I thank God everyday of my life. I moved and ended up leaving the VA due to car pooling situation. I didn't have a license at the time. I was jobless until a member at the church told me to put in an application as a dishwasher at a social club. I became the head washer because I did my job so well.

I met another man while working at the club. He was cook. We only saw each other was at night after work because he as still living with his daughter's mother. Another failed relationship. I had become a waitress and made the best of it. I met another man who was on crack. I didn't know that he was a user until one day he stole my money. He disappeared and I didn't here from him for a long time. I met him going to work. He returned and stated he was clean. I had my own car for the first time in my life I was driving. I was able to get back and forth to work. I had met another crack user which his sister didn't tell me, one day I was taking him somewhere far out and the sun blinded me I crashed into someone else and totaled my car and he left me stranded. I did get another car later. Will came back into the picture and things were going okay. My daughter didn't like him I found out later he was still on drugs when he stole my car and I had reported it stolen and thank God it was found. We never spoke and he never called again.

Paul called me one day out of the blue to see out how I was doing and tried to explain about his marriage. He was now having martial problems and he was going to get a divorce. My level of faith had increased and I really couldn't trust him anymore. After what happened really all I could do was pray for their marriage because I didn't want to be the one who caused him to leave his wife. I listened as a friend but what I should have done was told him he needed to speak with one of the deacons at his church or even his

Pastor. I know now that me being single at that time I had no right to discuss another man's marriage.

I probably would not have fallen back into that mood with Paul again. I allowed my flesh to take me right back to the same old spirit. Paul being who he was shouldn't have allowed it to happen. I ended up back into a relationship and it became worst. Being that I had just gotten my own house and moved in just before Christmas. Paul moved in the middle of the following year so I really never got to enjoy being in my first home along with my children by ourselves.

Paul moved in and you would have thought I would have help with my bills but I paid all. I came in from work, slept, and went to church. Paul's drinking became worst he was drowning all of his sorrow in a bottle of booze. I felt as though it was my fault for allowing myself to get involved with a married alcoholic preacher man with no ends. We stayed together throughout the whole time he was drinking then this habit started to rub off on me. One glass of wine every now and then turned into an everyday drink. I was still going to church but sinning the rest of the week neither one of us was helping each other. He was sinking badly and the wine was relaxing. The relationship was fading and one day Paul said he was moving that was a good thing but also bad.

After working at the String and Splinter for a while as a waitress one of the members suggested I go back to school so that I could broaden my education that I could become more than a waitress. Don't get wrong there is nothing wrong with being a waitress I just wanted more out of my life. Well I looked into it and

I started going to college in the evening but it became too much and I had to stop. I had to take on another job to help complete the bills. I took on another job at a Telecommunication company; this was an evening job. I went to the String and Splinter from 10am-3pm sometimes to 4pm and my evening shift went from 9pm-4am or 6pm-1am. I was offered a fulltime position that's when I left String and Splinter. Working for Phone Company gave me a great opportunity to advance and for me that was great. I always wanted to be in a job to grow within the company and that I did. I was transferred to collections then to Receptions working on applying payments to customer's accounts.

Paul moved out he moved to an area where a good friend of mine lived. Her mother had gotten him an apartment close to her, you see Paul and I joined the same church and we were attending like a family. Sarah's mother took to us very well and so did the pastor and church members. I was attending church with a man like we were one big happy family and I had never been invited to this home. One day my pastor came to be and dropped a subtle hint. He said "One day when you feel the urge to drive, just go ride around the neighborhood and check things out." I did just that.

I caught Paul coming out of Sarah's house getting into his car. I followed him to a drug store and confronted him and of course he lied. Another time I took that drive and this time I saw his car parked at her house at midnight. I knew what was going on. I rang the boor bell and he came out we started arguing. I still take responsibility for what happened because I allowed it from the beginning. Time passed and I went into a depression. Especially once I found out they were getting married. A girl I worked with from Phone Company told me how Sarah had been planning her wedding with Paul. I felt so hurt. Second time this man has done this to me. How naive could I be?

When I called him to confront him on his pending marriage he couldn't say anything. Not saying anything is worse than saying something. I thank God for the friends that worked with me helped me through my tough times. They would comfort me on the job and would come by my home for more comforting. We would sit and talk over dinner. They were my spiritual sisters and brother (Kerry, Barry, and Toni). At night when they were gone I was all alone and I cry all night long. All sorts of Gospel programs would come on I was hearing the word but not listening to what was being said. I wasn't eating but yet putting a front up for my children. I just didn't want them to see their mother in a certain way. I was still going to work my body was there the work was getting done but my heart was ripped out.

That November my family came down from Boston and Ruby brought my nephew, LaTrell, down for the first time. You see she was expecting twins but only one lived. I was so caught up in my own mess I couldn't be there for her. They arrived and I held that tiny baby in my arms my whole life changed within seconds. It was like I knew this child was going to need me and I had to come to terms with my life for him and I did just that. It's amazing how something or someone comes into to your life and makes you worth living again. Thanksgiving was a joyful time for us but when my family had to leave and return back to Boston I felt like I needed to be there with them. We made plans for me to come up for Christmas with the family and we did just that. It was good going home. I played with the baby the entire time I was there. I made a huge decision to move back to Boston for good. Just before I was ready to return to Boston would you believe that I met my soul mate.

About two and a half weeks before I was to leave for Boston; Bernard and I had our first date. I was trying to get over my relationship with Paul. He took me to Red Lobster which is my favorite restaurant until this day. It was a very nice evening we talked, ate, and found out that our birthdays were in the same month and one day after the other. He would call sometimes and we talked and on Sundays he would come by and pickup a plate of food.

Just before my children and I were about to leave for Boston my mother had a stroke. My plans to leave in the summer had been canceled and we made arrangements to leave in late March. I sold my furniture and told Bernard about my plans to leave NC. I hated to leave since we were getting to know each other but yet and still he was with someone. He always said he was in this situation only for a little while. Well at that time I didn't know but he said he would call every weekend and for me to do the same. I picked up the U-Haul and packed what we were going to take. I gave away a lot of stuff. My daughter Rea's boyfriend, Michael, whom she had been dating for years to my surprise, was moving with us. I had given my notice to all employment personnel and they really hated to see me go.

We left High Point early Saturday morning Tracey, Rea, and myself road with Michael in his car. David rode in the U-Haul with Moe's son. The trip was long and we rested when needed, ate, and gassed up until the U-Haul truck that was pulling my car got loose. We stopped at a rest area and waited for a maintained truck to fix it at one of the U-Haul service stations. Then we were back on the road to Boston. Upon arrival in New York Moe's son said we could stop by his aunt's house for directions from there. We did and had a twenty minute rest and got in Newton, MA. It was cold and we were hungry very aggravated.

We got settled that following Monday. I went to the Temp Agency they found me a job right away. I worked there for about a month or two until I was offered a job within the Temp Agency as a secretary. I was to process applications I really liked the job. I hadn't had time to date. I was really enjoying my nephew. He would call me mama and slept with me. The baby became so attached to me that I realized I had to try and give up smoking cigarettes. I didn't want LaTrell's lungs to get messed up from second hand smoke. Time passed and I was going to church on the regular.

One day while I was taking the train to my car I ran into Brian who was an old friend from my past. We exchanged phone numbers and talked a little and parted ways. Then one evening he called me and we talked more then made an arrangement to meet. I really wasn't looking for a relationship at this time. Brian and I went out several times. I met his grandmother saw the place where he was staying it wasn't what I expected of him. Who was I to judge? When I found out that Brian was on drugs that was a warning sign for me.

I backed off and left him alone. One morning after church service as I was leaving I saw an old face that I knew growing up in Mission Hill. We spoke and talked for a brief moment.

We exchanged numbers but I never called him. The week before Father's Day Jack called. I am all for giving a person a chance. Even though he had just got out of jail and was living in a half way house for men. We went out to the park I think; I do know I had invited him to dinner one Sunday. My mom didn't like him from the start but this time at least I thought I was doing things by the Word of God. He kept saying God told him to call me. Well dinner went fine and I drove him back to the half way house. Later that evening we talked more and started getting closer. This man had issues that kept arising. I really was trying to see this relationship through because I felt that he was in church and I thought God was going to honor this relationship. I was doing the right thing. If God did not ordain that relationship then it's not for you and you need to wait on him.

Many relationships go wrong because we women try to find a man because we don't want to be alone. My past experience told me it's better to be alone than abused. My mom always told me you can do bad all by yourself. So why do you need a man to help you do badly? Well this relationship was always on and off. There was a time when the family was getting together because LaTrell's father was coming into town. We were either going to cookout or go out to eat. Jack got very upset and started cursing me out. He called some nasty names that I won't mention but you can use your imagination.

That was a warning sign then to run and get out while you still can. I went on with my family, Jack called all that day wanting to argue until finally I said to leave me alone and hung the phone up. That next day he was at my job picking me up from work which he always did but this time he brought flowers. Yes, I was still mad and we talked while on the train all the way to the car. We even sat in my car and started arguing until I really started telling him we need to back up and go slow because I need time to heal from my hurt from Paul. Depression is a deadly thing and it's very important for you to allow yourself to heal. Please hear me women if you don't you will end up back into another relationship and be worst off then before.

I had to tell him I needed to go home because I was tired of arguing and we weren't getting anywhere. Jack called later that night and talked and talked unit I said we'll try again to make it work. He continued to pick me up from work throughout the relationship we continued to argue. I remember times when he called me every name in the book even down to a female dog. Well my family didn't like him and every time I would break it off he would bring gifts and be nice to me. The only thing that made me feel like I was in another place was when Bernard would call it always made my day. He was still going through the same relationship as before. Now in the mean time Jack and I were still dating until one day he brought me an engagement ring. Which I had been out all that night and came home to show my sister Ruby she said the ring was nice but when I told her who it was from she stated "I hoped I knew what I was doing." My mother on the other hand wasn't happy. We had so many problems until the day of the marriage. He took the ring back all the time.

One day I said just keep it I don't really care. While all this was going on I applied for a new job working for a big housing co. as the main receptionist for the office of development. I really liked this job a lot. The brokers and lawyers were very helpful and caring. This was the kind of job where in the evening I had to the key to lock the elevator at night. The area was nice as well as the scenery. Well needless to say I went through with the wedding. My life went down, by that time Bernard and I had stopped talking because he was still going through some things so I stopped calling. My sister and I shopped around looking for a dress for me and the bridesmaids.

You would think it would be a happy time looking for a dress and being together but for me I just kept asking myself was this really something I wanted to do. A month before the wedding I had moved in with him and things were bad. I felt trapped. It seemed like everything I did wasn't right he claimed I had been cheating and even accused me of calling other men names out in my sleep. I was being so naive and I believed him and even went to see a physiologist to talk to her about my problem. I didn't tell her what my boyfriend was saying and this had been going on throughout the whole time I moved in with him. There were times when my hair wasn't right and he accused me of messing around. It got to the point where he was checking my clothes for evidence. He would call me at work and accused me of making personal calls and cheating on him.

It was a strong hold and that goes back to spirits taking control and really I felt like I was doing the right thing by being a Christian, thinking it was what the Lord wanted. I really didn't like being alone. My problem was just being insecure about myself. Now that I have grown in Christ things are different I have confidence Philippians 4:13 says ' I can do all things in Christ which strengthens me ". I really was just a baby in Christ still on milk never really grew up or stepped out on faith. Well the day of the wedding I really felt in my heart it was still wrong. People in the church came to me to make sure I knew what I was doing that's when I should have spoken up.

I walked down the isle said my "I do's" and it was over. We had a beautiful reception then home. I felt like the same because I was already living there it never became home. Yet and still in the beginning when I got the ring there were times he would take it back just because he was mad and wanted to be in control. I had won a trip on a cruise so that's where we went. Our room was a good size it had separate beds and throughout the cruise we were like friends. He still claimed that I was calling out men names in my sleep. Now when I look back on that relationship he was very insecure about himself it had nothing to do with me.

While on the boat the bathroom got backed up and we were out on the water with a messy bathroom. Eventually the cruise had to be canceled which was fine with me. After returning back home life still hadn't got any better. We ended up moving and I really liked the apartment. I was on pills for depression. They had put me on two to three different types of anti-depressants. You see this man was trying to make me crazy and I didn't see or understand the type of abuse I was going through. There are all types of abuse Physical Abuse, Sexual Abuse, Psychological Abuse, Emotional or Verbal Abuse, and Economic Abuse. I was dealing with several abuses.

The medication prescribed to me was supposed to relief me from all kinds of depression. After moving into the apartment house things were going down fast. We would argue everyday about little things. Jack continued to take the ring back. I remember the last time he took it back I hurried up and gave it to him and told him to keep it. I knew I had to change my life, so I decided to join the choir and he joined too. It was like I couldn't get away from him not even for a little bit except for at my sister's house or when I went to get my hair done. Sometimes it would take until 10pm. I would have a lot of missed calls on my cell phone. I think he tried to intimidate me but it didn't work. One day we had a big argument and he stated yelling that "I was lucky that I'm not the way I used to be".

Now the threats were coming in. I got to work he called all day long it seemed like it was every hour or less. That night when I got home we still continued to argue. I know my kids didn't really like him so they never said anything to him and he never said anything to them. It was like he was invisible. The next day the kids were already gone to school and just as I was leaving we had another argument. I had been sleeping in the living room on the floor because I was told not to sleep on his couch. The argument got really heated and he hit the wall it missed me just by and inch. That's when I really made up my mind and went to get a restraining order against him.

It took my entire lunch break but I had to get it done because I was afraid for my life. That night my sister came back home with me and two officers came and picked him up he was very angry and stated that the section 8 voucher was in his name. Then we went to court and I won the case. Jack stayed away for a while but kept calling and not saying nothing just breathing on the phone. One day when he called and I sat and listened that was a big mistake but to me it didn't make a difference because I had a restraining order in affect. That started an uproar he called my job all day long then we went to court again.

I remember one day I was sitting in the park outside from the job. I just gave up and let him move back in with a restraining order still in affect. This is when a lot of women who go through abuse allow the abuser to get back into their lives. When this happens they can end up worst then before or even dead. I had took on another job as a dispatcher it fit my morning schedule. I would finish my day job come home cook take care of the household issues then sleep until it was time to go to my night job which was from 12am till 6am. I really liked the job very much and it helped with the bills and many other things. First things were going good we met with the new pastor of the church and talked to him about helping us get on the right track. It worked for about a month or two, and then things started to go back to the way they were.

Jack decided to get baptized, we thought it would help change the relationship for the better but it didn't. A member of the church told me later that day that you go into the water and come up the same with no change. So, in other words you did it just for show.

Trying to perpetrate but you are just going through the motions. Eventually all the covers are pulled off and you are seen for the person you really are, which was a wolf in sheep's clothing. Our problems continued and got even worst. I was still going to work at my evening job and back to sleeping on the living room floor.

I awoke to find a completely nude man standing at the end of the hall in the doorway. It was like he was hypnotized. He was just standing with no movement at all. It was so strange it got me to thinking what was going on and why was he doing that. I kept telling myself I made a huge mistake for letting him come back. There was a time he would walk to church because he didn't want to ride in the car with me. The men in the parking lot looked and you could tell they were like what was his problem. No, the restraining order was not taking off it was pending for a year until it was time to re-evaluate the circumstances.

Jack found himself out of the church spirit when he would see any man talk to me. His jealousy was very unbecoming. You see he was trying to keep me confined sometimes an abuser doesn't want to share you with anyone. I dreamed that something bad happened to one of my children and I awoke to a disturbing phone call.

My dream had come to life. My child called to tell me that she was touched while sleeping. All I could think was that this had to be a dream. I called my oldest daughter to go pick up her brother and sister and take Tracey to the hospital. Jack got on the phone while my child was crying and kept saying what's wrong. Now I got to thinking why did he pick up the phone he didn't know I was on it or did he? I called management to cover and left for the hospital. We waited for a long time I knew they had contacted social service because it was procedure.

While at the hospital Jack kept leaving messages on my cell phone wanting to know what was going on. After we left the hospital my sister told my child to go home with her. Rose and I and went to the police station to give a report. I called my job and told them what was going on they were very understanding. They offered help and said let them know if I needed anything. Later that evening my sister and I went to pickup some clothes because we were going to stay with her for a while. My nights were days and days were nights at times I really didn't know if 1 was coming or going. I kept going over it in my head and was wondering what was it I did wrong. Could it have been I worked too much and how long had he been doing this?

I really had to trust in the Lord with all thine heart and lean not on thine own understanding. (Proverbs 3:5) It took a while for me to really focus on my life again. Eventually I went back to work it seemed I cried more but thank God for my job because they were really there for me. The third day I was back at work one of the lawyers asked me what I wanted to do. That's when I said to get a divorce and from that point they handled everything. While I was at work he would call and say very ugly things. We were to take a family vacation to Virginia then on to High Point, NC to see my grandmother.

This was a well needed trip. It relieved both of our minds until the trial started. The whole family had a great time. Once we got to High Point we checked into a hotel changed and went to see my grandmother. I was driving the rental van back to the hotel when I saw Bernard. He gave me his phone number and came by to see us later that day. He was still in the same situation but this time we would keep in contact. I didn't get to see him before we left but did call and promised to call from now on. We headed back to Boston, the moment I arrived the harassment started.

There were so many ugly messages on the phone I had to erase them. Jack really showed out at church on Sunday. He started arguing while I was going out the door. First, he tried to talk to me while in the choir stand but one of the choir members didn't allow him too. So as we left he started saying all sorts of bad things as the parking lot attendant tried to tell him to move on because of the restraining order. Since I never lifted it off even though I allowed him to come back in my home he still had to stay away from me until the re-evaluation day.

Jack accused me of sleeping with one of the married parking attendants along with everyone else. This man really needs help. Anyone that is insecure about his life is not a person you want to get involved with. The harassment really didn't stop there he continued to call the house and called me everything except a child of God. This time I got smart and instead of erasing the voice messages I called 911 and had them listen to the messages. That following week a woman from social services came by. She made me feel so degraded. She checked my refrigerator and cabinets for food. She checked the bedrooms and talked to each of my children. I understand she had a job to do but made me feel like I was a bad parent when my only crime was loving my children and putting my life back together. I had nothing to hide there was food and the house was clean. It was good on my behalf that I went to the police station right after we left the hospital it was a wise decision.

The child protection woman told me that she was assigned to the case and suggested we seek counseling. Well we tried that and my child became very defensive and all she kept saying was that she wanted this to be over and for everyone to leave her alone. When the trial came it was a very tense day for me. First, they had my child go in and tell what happened while they asked her questions. My job provided the attorney for me I remembered one of the managers called me into his office and talked with me about everything. My job took care of everything from the fees to making sure time wasn't taken due to lawyer appointments. After my child was finished testifying it was time for me to go in they wanted to know why I didn't tell Jack what was wrong with my child and why I was taking them out of the house. I said I did what I had to do in order to protect her.

The judge ruled in favor of my child and commended me on how I didn't do like most parents and not listen to my child. Children are a blessing in the Old Testament some women were barren and in this time as well you have so many that want children and cannot have any.

My lawyer worked on the divorce. I got that done with no problem. I went on trying to put my life back together and focused on church. I met an Evangelist there. She always gave me a good word of encouragement, but one day she said something that made me feel a whole lot better. She told me that God loves me very much and that I had been looking for love in all the wrong places and it was always staring me right in my face, John 16:9-13 says and from that day forth my heart truly love thy father, Jesus gave his life for me. One night a week the Evangelist taught a class I really loved going there you learn a whole lot each week.

Then one day she was ordained. We had been having so much problems at the church since the Bishop died, so many arguments issue after issue. People were mad because they were not next in line as pastor. So, I started attending bible study in Pastor's home every Wednesday. I remained faithful to the church. I had been a member from the time I left NC. I talked to Bernard off and on but he still was in his situation. Bernard finally became free of his situation. He called and said he paved the driveway for me and he wanted me to come home. I planned my vacation for July weekend 2004. Tracey didn't want to go for the visit but David and I did. I had a great time. He proposed over the phone. We knew that we had some love for each other but just couldn't be together. I took the train down we got there late.

He had to go to work but later that evening we talked for along time. During the next two days he placed my engagement ring on my finger. While we stayed there I did a lot of cleaning and throwing out things that were no longer needed. That 4th weekend Bernard took me over his mom's house and everything went well. He announced our engagement and everyone was happy. His mother asked for my phone number so we could plan the wedding. They set the date for September 23.

2001. I really didn't have a lot of time. I was moving the end of August so I could register David for school. Soon I had to leave and return back to Boston.

When I got back I told my family but no one was happy they all wanted to know why I had to go back to North Carolina. I returned back down south and got married, we went on a cruise for our honeymoon we had a great time. Now I have a wonderful husband my three beautiful children and two grandchildren that are blessings. I have a wonderful pastor and I am an Evangelist and I do Women Seminars each year or as the Lord lead me too. Now I know that there is always light at the end of the tunnel like the scripture says," when I sit in darkness the Lord shall be a light unto me" Micah 7:8.

"INSIDE OUT"

Then along came Jesus who knew my sight, He said cast all my cares unto him for he cared for me. He opened my heart and took away the dark. He cleansed all my sins so that I could be made whole again. My life is now turned about because now I have been made whole from inside out

Evangelist Mary Quick

Understanding Domestic Violence

Domestic violence defined

Domestic violence is chronic abuse by one current or former intimate partner against the other. It is characterized by a pattern of coercive control and increasing entrapment. The partners can be married, divorced, separated, living together, or having an ongoing intimate relationship, or they could have previously been involved in such a relationship. The partners can be heterosexual or homosexual. The intimate context of the violence is important in understanding the nature of the problem and in developing effective interventions. The intimate context of domestic violence shapes the way in which both the perpetrator and the victim relate to and outside the relationship to take domestic violence less seriously than other types of violence (Gangly 1995).

Abuse tactics

Batterers use a variety of abuse tactics to dominate and maintain control over their partners. They may attempt to manipulate every aspect of their partners' lives. Unchallenged, men who batter learn that violence is an acceptable and effective way to resolve problems and get what they want. Many battered women report that the physical violence is not as damaging as the relentless emotional and psychological abuse that cripples and isolates them. In general abuse tends to increase in frequency and severity over time. Here are examples of abusive behaviors. Many batterers:

Physical abuse

Inflict or attempt to inflict physical injury by grabbing, pinching, shoving, slapping, punching, hitting with blunt objects

Use or threaten to use a gun or other weapon

Withhold access to resources necessary to maintain health such as food, sleep, medication, medical care, or a wheelchair

Force alcohol or other drug use

Sexual abuse

Rape

Force sexual contact including fondling, sodomy, bestiality, sex with others, unprotected sex

Force use of pornography

Attempt to undermine the victims' sexuality by treating them in a sexually derogatory manner

Psychological abuse

Frighten their partners by intimidating, menacing, stalking, blackmailing, harassing, harming pets or property, or by threatening physical harm to self, victim, children or others

Isolate or attempt to isolate their partners' personal relationships by harassing others, constantly "checking up, "and making unfounded accusations

Imprison their partners

Emotional or verbal abuse

Undermine or attempt to undermine their partners' sense of self-worth through constant criticism, belittling their abilities and competencies, insulting them, or withdrawing from them

Manipulate their partners' feelings and emotions to induce guilt

Subvert their partners' relationship with the children

Make unwarranted accusations of infidelity

Repeatedly make and break promises

Economic abuse

Make or attempt to make their partners financially dependent by maintaining total control over financial resources including their partners' earned income or resources including public assistance or social security

Withhold money and/or assess to money

Forbid attendance at school or work

Harass their partners' job

Require justification for all money spent

Force welfare fraud

Withhold information about family finances

Run up bills for which their partners are responsible for payment

A Grandma Plea "

Somebody prayed for me
Hoping one day that I might be able to see
Somebody prayed for me
While I was sleeping in my sin
Somebody prayed for me
Because I still was letting hell come in
They prayed that I may soon come out
And never ever had a doubt
Somebody prayed for me
You see this was my grandma's plea
She prayed for me because she always believed
Somebody prayed for me.

Evangelist Mary Quick

About the Author

Mary Quick was born Mary Yvonne Grice to Dollie and William Grice in Philadelphia, PA. She is the oldest of five children. She graduated from Madison Park High School. She attented Beacon College. She moved from Boston, MA to High Point,NC where she met her husband Everette Bernard Quick of five years. They now reside in Thomasville, NC. They have three childern Aja Grice,Shatrece Whitfield, and David Grice they have two grandchildern Jakai Whitfield and Jazmine Kidd, and soon another to be added.

Mary Quick is an Evangelist of the Gospel. Mary attends Living Epistle Bible College where she has received her Associate Degree and she is now there for her Bachelors. Her favorite scripture is Psalms 37: 1-6.